NONPERISHABLE

The Story of One Woman's Determination
to Find Hope; Beat The Odds
And Create Her Own Successful Path

By

LAKEISHA HINNANT

As Told to
Mary E. Davis, Ghost Writer
© 2015

NONPERISHABLE

By

LAKEISHA HINNANT

**As told to
Mary E. Davis, Ghost Writer**

Dedication

To my mom, Angela Lee
and my grandmother, Linda Lee.
Thank you for showing me the value of hard work
and to always want and strive for the best from life.

Thanks to my grandfather, Cleveland Lee
and my dad, Vincent Scott
for always being there for me.

Thanks to Hope Revels, my best friend,
And her parents, Brenda & Dennis Revels,
for their unwavering support.

Thanks also to my wonderful brothers,
Vincent Scott & Mical Scott,
For always supporting me.

Thanks to my family and friends
For their love and support.

The greatest wealth of all
Comes not from money,
But through the love we share.
And it comes not
From what we get in life,
But through what we give.

CONTENTS

Chapter 1
More Than A Statistic

One of 3,913,000 babies born in the United States in 1988, I was among the 26-percent of newborns born to single mothers in that year. More specifically still, I was one of 63-percent of newborn black babies born to single American mothers. But I was one of just a few babies born in the U.S. to young unwed mothers. These statistics may forever be a part of the demography of American motherhood in 1988, but they would, in no way, define me, hinder me nor hold me back, in the coming years.

My start could be considered dismal and bleak, by some people, since statistics show that nearly 80-percent of babies born to teen mothers end up in poverty and on welfare. While it could be said that 'the odds were against me' from the start, I never felt that way in the least; nor was I even aware that history, statistics or expectations of anything less than 'my very best' even existed. For me, life would simply always be 'what I made of it' and 'what I put it into it.'

Since my mother was just a teenager, she was still a child herself at the time of my birth. Fortunately, my grandmother raised me from the time

I was a newborn and years later, I went back and forth, between my mother's and my grandmother's homes in Tampa, Florida.

Mine was a fairly typical childhood, but two things were always made very clear to me: '*Education is the key to success in all things* and *anything less than my best was simply not good enough.*' While I was always a very good student, the only thing that got me into trouble was the fact that I was so talkative in class. Both my grandmother and my mom always re-inforced the importance of education and I knew they *didn't play* when it came to my grades.

One day, I came home from school, to my grandmother's house, with my report card in-hand. My academic grades were good, but I had a bad mark in conduct, and so I knew what was coming when my mother arrived a short while later.

"Lakeisha, I didn't raise you like this!" Mom yelled at me. "I didn't raise you to misbehave in front of others!"

I looked down at the floor and swallowed hard. I'd fully expected the lashing and the disappointment in my mother's voice.

"I'll do better," I promised.

"You'd better!" she added. "You're better than this!"

That would be my first realization that just being smart wasn't enough in this world. I knew on that day that my behavior and my actions would create my reputation; and that if I wanted to have a good one, then it would be up to me. I learned that even as children, we are judged by oth-ers, so it' important to give them good things on which to judge us. As the Bible says in Proverb 20:11, "Even a child is known by his doings," so I decided that it is never too early to do my best. This would hold true, not just in my youth, but into adulthood too, as I'd learn that a positive reputation is invaluable in all aspects of life, both personal and profes-sional.

Like most kids, I watched my mother and my grandmother, as examples in my life of how women behave and I naturally formed some assumptions and expectations for myself. As a young teen, I clung to the idea that I'd most likely become a registered nurse, like my mom had done.

Later on, following a slight detour on the road to a career in medicine, I decided to go to Pharmacy Tech School, following my mom's suggestion. "You can get a grant to go school," Mom told me.

She was right and I qualified for the grant and started classes. I didn't particularly like it though and it didn't hold my interest. Halfway through the course, I'd earned a score of 83-percent on a test that had required a minimum score of 86-percent, in order to continue on to the next phase in the program. My heart just hadn't been in it and I knew it deep down in my soul. In fact, I felt relieved when I'd learned that I hadn't passed the important exam and that I'd have to wait a year in order to take the test again.

Instead of a pharmacy career, I decided that I'd go to school to become a teacher. When I wasn't in class, I worked at a retail job in the local Sally's Beauty Supply store in town. Later, during Christmas Break, I switched to online classes that I took from home. Although I did well in my classes, something still didn't feel right to me. While I was going to school and working toward a goal, it somehow didn't feel like 'the best fit' for me and I grew restless as I tried to figure out what I should do with my life. It seemed to me that school takes such a long time to complete and I was ready to get out into the world and to start living my life. In my eyes, the world was filled with exciting possibilities and interesting things just waiting to be discovered and I was antsy to jump right into it!

My goals, my dreams and my aspirations all seemed to align one day as I talked with my friend, Hope, about how I'd been feeling. I knew Hope always seemed happy, fulfilled and like she enjoyed her life, so what she said really made sense to me.

"There's nothing like it!" Hope told me. "It's great money; I love what I do and I get to travel every single day!"

"But semi-trucks?" I laughed. "I don't know if I could drive something that *big*!"

"You can learn," she explained. "No one knows how to drive a rig until they're taught. And you're smart! It'll be a breeze for you!"

I'd always been in awe of the big semis on the road. It had always fascinated me to watch when I'd pulled-up next to one at a traffic light or had passed on the highway. They were huge, powerful and in control; and yet the drivers were obviously skilled, careful and highly trained. It was a mixture that quietly, yet politely, demanded respect from the other drivers. The possibilities intrigued me as I thought for a few days about the conversation I'd had with Hope.

I did a little research about the trucking industry and learned that, according to the American Trucking Association, there existed a shortage of nearly 30,000 drivers across the nation. And although trucking is generally perceived as a male-dominated industry, things are definitely changing. In 2000, women made up 4.7% of the US trucking payroll, but their jobs were usually in sales, dispatch, marketing or recruiting positions. Today though, according to recent labor statistics, just over 5-percent of the drivers *on the road* are **women**.

Chapter 2
The Power of Passion

The first woman to earn her Commercial CDL and drive a commercial vehicle was Lillie McGee Drennan and she earned this distinction in 1929, the year that would also have its place in American history as the start of The Great Depression. And at a time when the US population was 120-million, Lillie Drennan would stand out as a woman who paved her way and made her own rules. This was no small feat either, because at the time Lillie drove, the trucks were designed for big men, and had heavy clutches and big gearshifts.

Lillie may have had a feminine-sounding name, but she was known to hold her own amongst male drivers, and in a time when women were not welcomed in the heavily male-dominated industry. She carried a revolver with her at all times and she eventually earned the respect of her male counterparts while she opened the doors for more women drivers.

After her time behind the wheel of a big rig, Lillie eventually became the sole owner of Drenne Truck Line, the first woman-owned trucking company in the United States. Some of the very male drivers who had once jeered and taunted her would become her employees and grow to respect their female boss.

Just like Lillie Drennan, the open road, and the income potential of trucking, held a certain allure for me too. The more I thought about Hope's suggestions, the more I began to visualize myself behind the wheel of a big rig, high above the other cars on the road, as I skillfully changed gears and maneuvered my own semi through traffic and along highways. I began to realize that it excited me to anticipate all the new destinations, new people and new experiences that I'd have if I followed Hope's suggestion.

"I can do this!" I decided one day as I looked-up information on my computer about the next CDL training classes being offered in Tampa. But I not only needed a Commercial Driver's License; I needed to learn to drive a *semi* too. The thought of the studying and coursework didn't scare me in the least. It was the intimidation of a big rig that I had to overcome in my own mind.

I found that Roadmaster Drivers School in Tampa offered a class that would teach me to drive a truck in three to four weeks. Through instruction and hands-on experience, Roadmaster's instructors would teach me to drive a semi and from what I'd read, it appeared that there would be a trainer to help me from the moment I walked in their door until they introduced me to my first employer. As I envisioned what to expect, I grew a little more comfortable with the possibility that I could actually learn to drive a big semi, just like Hope and just like all the drivers I'd seen on the roadways.

"You want to do WHAT?" my mom asked when I told her my plans. "But I thought you wanted to finish school and become a teacher," my grandma added.

"I've changed my mind," I explained. "I'm doing this!"

Just like always, I knew I'd get out of truck driving school what I was willing to put into it. I made up my mind to give it my all and to never lose sight of my goal!

As it turned out, Roadmasters Drivers School is located on the Florida State Fairgrounds in Tampa, near the Hard Rock Casino. For me, this was nearby; but for people who came from out of town, they could spend time at the casino or at Busch Gardens or watching local sporting events, when not in class. I preferred to spend my time reading and studying so I'd be ready for my tests.

In addition to classroom work, students got extensive hands-on training at a 27-acre driving school training course that had been specially constructed for tractor-trailer driving instruction. On one hand, it was a comfort to know I'd be able to practice in a controlled environment, as I got the feel of a semi. But, on the other hand, I found I'd have to overcome a few unexpected obstacles and hurdles *not* found on the driving course.

Besides my self, there was just one other woman in my class at Roadmasters. JoAnne was 54; and she and I were the only two women in our class of thirty students.

The 1960s saw more women drivers entering the trucking industry than any other time in US history. Years ago though, conditions were tough for those women who dared reach for more than a 'desk job' within a trucking company. Women were not made to feel welcome in the perceived 'man's world' of trucking. The working conditions created obstacles too. At that time, truck stops didn't even provide women's restrooms. In order to simply take a quick shower, a female driver had to chain the restroom door shut and have someone 'stand guard' outside the door.

Even the trucking unions made life hard on female drivers in the early days. Male drivers and the unions never cut the females any slack and they made it difficult at times for females whenever they could. Women are fortified, strong souls though, and those ladies who persevered in the beginning made it easier for the females who came after them.

I knew JoAnne and I would persevere too, and that we'd earn our CDLs – no matter what. The class size soon dwindled though, as students dropped-out for one reason or another. A few people had failed their mandatory drug tests; some didn't pay their required tuition or fees and others still, had simply found the class was too hard or that it just 'wasn't for them.' As the class grew smaller and there were eventually just 16 students left, it became easier for the instructors to focus on those of us whom were left.

"Lakeisha, you're just too girly!" Mike, my instructor, laughed one day. "You need to go back to school and do something else. This isn't for you!"

"I've got this," I told him.

Moments later, I found myself in the bathroom and in tears. I splashed some water on my face and looked at my 22-year old reflection in the mirror over the sink.

"God, help me," I prayed. "Help me to do this! Be with me and guide me. Give me the strength to make it through!"

I took a deep breath and then dried my face with a paper towel. By the time I opened the bathroom door again, I felt refreshed, strengthened and more determined than ever. With my back straight and my head held high, I went back to our group.

"You've *got* this, girl!" I told myself when I rejoined my class of fifteen.

Mike continued to berate me, harangue me and try his best to persuade me to quit. The more he tried though, the more determined I became to prove him wrong about the fortitude of the young, feminine 'girly girl.'

When the day came for me to practice some specific maneuvers behind the wheel of the semi, I was nervous, just like most of the other students. But unlike the other students, I had Mike's watchful eyes on me, and just hoping I'd give up, quit and prove him right. I had some problems backing-up the big rig. After a few attempts, I got out of the driver's seat to give someone else is turn.

"Lakeisha, just give it up, girl!" Mike said. "Maybe you should just get your *B License* and call it a day!"

Getting a 'B License' wouldn't give me as many options or career opportunities though, and I knew it. There are three types of licenses issued by the Department of Motor Vehicles. Most people have a Class C License, which allows them to drive any vehicle, as long as it weighs less than 26,000 pounds. A Class B License allows the holder to drive farm labor vehicles, buses or any car or trailer under 45-feet in total length. A 'B License' would not allow me to pull a trailer that weighed over 10,000 pounds, which would limit my possibilities – and my income potential. I knew that I had to obtain my *A License*.

"No way, Mike!" I replied. "I'm not *leaving* here without my *A License!*"

For my whole life, I'd been the kind of person who'd gone out of my way to prove to people that I could do what I wanted. I'd never been afraid of hard work and I'd always refused to let others tell *me* what I could and could not do with my own life. Mike's attitude seemed to me like just one more obstacle that I'd have to overcome. It was as if he were a pesky little speed-bump that might slow me down, ever so briefly, but then I'd roll right over him and be on my way again, never looking back at him in my side-view mirrors.

When it was my turn again, I confidently climbed up into the driver's seat of the semi, adjusted my seat, fastened my seatbelt and positioned my side mirrors. With the practiced skill of an old pro, I performed the required backing maneuver – *one, two, three* – and then I silently turned off the engine, opened the door and climbed down again. It felt good to face my discomfort, overcome it and triumphantly move on to the next step! It had been the same way that I'd always conquered anything in my life – *one step at a time* and with a 'can do' attitude.

Truck driving school wasn't difficult in it *self*, although it was made more difficult by the negative attitude of our instructor. And while I knew I'd be disappointed if I were to fail the course, I was certain that the bigger disappointment for me would be in myself. I'd always been the kind of girl who'd hear, "You can't," and I'd immediately respond with, "Just WATCH me!"

I've always been convinced that the biggest reason people don't try new things or difficult things is that they have a deep-seated 'fear of failure.' To some people, they'd simply rather not try new things, if there exists the slightest chance they might fail. But, life is too short to sit on the sidelines and observe! Instead of worrying about failing, or about what others think, I prefer to throw that energy into growing, learning and bettering myself. That's exactly what I did during the truck driver's training course.

As the only women in our class, JoAnne and I encouraged one another throughout our training program. Although she was old enough to be my mother – in fact, she was 18 years *older* than my *own* mother – I knew JoAnne was my silent cheerleader. And I knew that we each wanted the other to make it and to prove Mike wrong, both for our selves and for other women, in general. Women are strong and our determination can be fierce; and I used these things to my advantage.

At the end of the training course, and after I'd taken my final exam, I saw Mike outside the school one day. He looked surprise to see me.

"I passed!" I grinned as I waved my certificate in the air.

Mike looked shocked, but I was filled with pride. It felt good to know I'd joined the ranks of over 150,000 female truck drivers in the United States!

Gone are the days of the image of the typical truck driver as a big, burly, tough-talking man. It's not just a 'man's world' anymore! Many women have recognized that there are many benefits for them too, in truck driving. Just like our male counterparts, women want higher pay and job security; and trucking offers just that. Studies show that women who choose non-traditional careers, like truck driving, often garner significantly higher salaries than women within traditionally female-dominated occupations. And just like men, women also enjoy independence through trucking jobs; and they also have the freedom to travel and experience new places and new people, while earning a great living at the same time.

After I'd completed my schooling and my hands-on training, it felt good to know I'd passed the course. But there was still much to be done and I knew I couldn't rest or lose my momentum.

Chapter 3
Eternal Education

Fortunately for me, my best friend, Hope, had already been driving for about five years. Since she had a job as a driver for Werner Enterprises, I'd spent time riding along with her, which gave me some invaluable 'on the road' experience. After I'd ridden along with Hope for the required 270-hours, she and I decided to partner and drive together as a team.

Hope and I worked well together; we made a great team and as best friends, we truly loved the time we spent together. Things were going great for us and I loved driving my big rig with my best friend beside me.

But, as we continued to faithfully pick-up and deliver our scheduled loads, Hope and I couldn't help but wonder how much *more* money we could make if we were to venture out on our own. While life was great, both Hope and I still wanted more. Since we saw the bills of lading and the figures on the invoices, we began to crunch the numbers and it became clear to both of us what we had to do.

In April 2014, *2 Women & A Rig, LLC* was born! Our company mantra is '*The World is Ours;*' and I love the possibilities that through trucking, we'll get to keep discovering new places, new people and unique experiences! If I had a typical office job, 'my world,' day after day, would only be what's on the other side of my office window; and *that* just doesn't excite me.

When we started our business, it was exactly a year, to the month, since I'd lost my beloved grandmother in April 2013; and while I'd wished she were still here to see what I've accomplished, I know in my heart that *she knows*. It's to her credit that I'd found the courage to stay focused and to 'stay the course' when things had gotten tough.

When we lost Grandma, I'd expected to be the most overwrought and emotional family member, since I'd been so close to her. But after she'd died, I found that I was more determined than ever to live my own life and to make my life the best it can be. Grandma's death made me think about my own mortality and what I really wanted out of my life, in the time that I've got.

I'd watched my grandmother work hard for many years. She'd been a woman of principle and a fine example of how to live a good life by doing the right things. Grandma was responsible, went to work, had a nice home and enjoyed nice things. For 34 years, Grandma worked hard, until one day, her job suddenly ended.

As much as I'd loved and adored Grandma, watching her life be changed, without her permission, gave me a hard and fast lesson that I'd never forget. I'd do everything in my power to keep control over my own life. (Though I didn't know it at the time, years later that would mean owning my own company and controlling my own destiny.)

Thanks to my grandmother, I'd had the love and guidance of positive female role model. Before life changed for her, Grandma had been a lead CNA, or Certified Nurse's Assistant, at a nursing home. When I was a pre-teen and a young teenager, she'd allowed me to accompany her to the home and to volunteer there. I did simple tasks, like passing out graham crackers and refilling patients' water glasses; and I sometimes played board game with some of the elderly residents. It provided me a great opportunity to learn about people, develop empathy and form a respectful admiration for my elders and all they can teach us.

Since I'd always enjoyed school and was a good student, I easily formed a close friendship with Mrs. Robinson, a resident of the home, who was a former school teacher. After school, I'd rush over to the nursing home, eager to see Mrs. Robinson and talk with her about what I'd learned that day. For three years, she was a constant figure in my life and someone whose company I enjoyed. I'd always presumed that Mrs. Robinson must have been a wonderful mother to her own two daughters and one son, since she seemed to be such a genuine and caring woman.

One day, after school, I went to the home, as always, eager to share my latest news. After tossing my book bag under a counter at the nurse's station, I went to Mrs. Robinson's room, just as I'd done hundreds of times before.

I stopped in my tracks though, the moment I got to her door's threshold. The door was open, her bed was stripped of all its linens and Mrs. Robinson's things were no longer all around the little room. It was as if her very essence had been wiped away and the room was still, silent and cold.

"Honey, she died this morning," a nurse said from behind me as she passed by the empty room.

I thought for a moment that my heart had stopped as I tried to catch my breath as the nurse's words sunk in. The finality of those words echoed in my head. "Died. This. Morning. Died. This. Morning."

Over our three years together, I'd come to love Mrs. Robinson and to realize that we don't have to be related by blood in order to call others 'our family' or to 'love them.' Mrs. Robinson had been special to me and I was sure she'd known it. After she'd gone, I wondered whom I'd talk with about my classes, my friends, my projects and life in general, since she was gone. Mrs. Robinson had always been there, waiting for me, smiling and purely happy to see me. I knew that day her loss would be something huge and defining in my life. What I *didn't* realize then, was that I'd always remember so many of Mrs. Robinson's 'lessons' and all she'd taught me during our regular visits.

In addition to my mother and my grandmother, Mrs. Robinson had also taught me that nothing is more important or more valuable than an education. "Stay in school, child!" she'd said, time and time again, as she looked me square in the eye. "I'm not telling you this because I was a teacher either; it's because I know life and life is easier when you're *educated*. And don't you be getting *boy crazy* either! There's plenty of time for that later on! Right now though, you stay focused on school, Lakeisha! Nothing's more important! Nothing! You hear me?"

Mrs. Robinson had been a wise teacher all her life, even long after she'd left her classroom. In time, I realized how and why she'd known the value and the importance of education – it's because it *never ends* and we must always continue to learn if we are to grow as people in this life.

I would learn, over time, that education is not always comfortable or easy, but it is always necessary. Some lessons are simple, while others may be painful; and yet *all* lessons are equally important in the end.

Like a body of water that doesn't flow or move, people, too, will become stagnant and putrid if they are not exposed to new things, new ideas and new information. This is so no matter what industry we serve and no matter at what point we may be in our careers. In order to get the ideas and the inspirations flowing again, people need only to get out of their comfort zones and to immerse themselves in 'life.' After all, both Grandma and Mrs. Robinson made it clear that 'all education does not come from the *pages of a textbook*.'

Chapter 4
'You Work All the Time!'

Since statistics are important and they are often accurate predictors of future outcomes, it is only natural that one's family might expect them to be like other family members, get a job, punch a clock, and fall in line with many typical households and family dynamics. With 9.75 million self-employed people in the US today, in comparison to the population of 326 million, it's clear that most people choose to be an employee, as opposed to being a business owner.

We're all individuals, we all have different goals, come from unique circumstances and have various priorities and expectations. There are definitely pros and cons to being an entrepreneur, just like there are in being an employee. Everyone must consider the positives and negatives of both scenarios when evaluating whether to 'take the plunge' into entrepreneurship. It's a very personal decision, although it still affects others within one's own family and social circles.

Hope and I are both cognizant of the fact that my siblings watch us, and take their cues from us and what they see us do in life. We take this very seriously, because we want to be positive examples to them as they make decisions about their own futures.

Hope's parents are very proud of their daughter, and only child, and her accomplishments and they fully support Hope and her dreams. While their support is important to her, Hope still loves being a business owner for what it brings to *her* and how it enhances *her* life – the true test of an *entrepreneur at heart.*

Being an entrepreneur is a very personal thing, and something one wants to their very core. Over time, I've learned to put aside the opinions of others, and to focus on what *I* want out of life and what's important to *me*. If I'm happy, and I'm doing well, then that's all that counts in my heart.

Sometimes I feel like people may not understand me, the reason I work so much and so hard, or my innate desire to succeed. We're all different though, and I respect their right to have their own opinions and their own lives, as they may fit into their personal plans. But I like the challenge of 'making my own success' and 'carving my own path' in life.

There's something so gratifying about working for myself and being directly responsible for how well I do in life. While this is precisely what some people find *scary, even terrifying,* about entrepreneurship, it's **exactly** what business owners find to be *exhilarating*!

"But you work ALL the time," people have said to me. "You never come around here anymore."

"I've got responsibilities," I honestly explain. "My job doesn't end at 5:00 now. It's my life! And if I'm going to get ahead, I've got to keep moving! No one gets anyplace by standing still!"

Everyone doesn't have the same mindset, and that's okay. My days are spent working on my business, building our brand, cementing our reputation within the industry and trying to get ahead. I just keep my focus and keep my eye on the prize.

Again, all lessons aren't easy, but they're all still equally important. Long ago, I decided that I couldn't let the opinions of others get in my way or bring me down.

I still don't think some people understand me or my goals and my desire to get ahead in life. But I know what I want out of life, and that's what counts.

Since losing Grandma, I now realize that life is short; and I prefer to 'live and let live' and to 'celebrate our differences' rather than to defend my own positions and choices. I'm happy with what I do, I love working for myself and I enjoy a great life, since I get out of it, what I put into it.

Sometimes I used to isolate myself when I didn't feel accepted by some people. What I know today though, is that entrepreneurs *are* different, and that's what makes them what they are in life – so it's really an advantage.

As I've slowly evolved and gotten a little older, I've come to realize that we don't have to all be alike; and our differences are what makes life interesting. We can love and respect one another for our similarities, as well as our differences.

In my world, every day is an opportunity and every day counts. I choose not to waste a single day, or even an hour; and to make the most of my time, as I try to find the balance in my evolving and exciting world of entrepreneurship.

I want my own teenaged brothers to see what a big world there is out there; and to know that it's *theirs* for the taking, if they're willing to educate themselves, find their focus and work for what they want in this world. Life, just like business, is pretty much about 'cause and effect' in most things. I've tried to show my younger brothers that if they 'work hard and do the right things,' that they will cause themselves to be elevated as people, which will positively affect their lives positively, and give them the desired effects of a great life.

It's always my goal to show them as much of life as I possibly can; to broaden their horizons and to inspire them to 'reach a little further' in all they do. I want the best for my brothers and I've made it my mission to help them any way I can.

"Anyone can have a job and most people need a *job* of some sort," I explained to my brothers one day. "But not everyone can run a business. There's a difference. And with that difference, comes responsibility, but also *endless* fantastic opportunities."

My *job* is 'running my company,' and I am an employee of my corporation. The company is a separate entity unto itself. My *job* is to grow the business, build my brand and provide the best service possible in the process.

When Hope and I started our trucking company, we didn't have all the answers – and we don't claim we have all the answers today either – because life is fluid and moving and ever changing, as we continue learning how to live in it. What we had, and what we do still *have*, is the burning desire to succeed and to be the best we can be, one step at a time. We don't mind working harder than the next guy either, if it means we'll get ahead. *THAT* mindset is what separates business owners from employees, and what separates a 'job' from a 'business.'

In our business, every day is different, and that's what we love about it! We get to see new places, meet new people and make new discoveries, one mile at a time. Since each day is different, some days present certain obstacles and unexpected hurdles. Like anything in life, when we're presented with a problem, we find a way to get through it, go over it or remove the hurdle altogether. As a business owner, I prefer to have the flexibility to step out of my comfort zone, make decisions, and have control of my own life. Someone recently asked if I had any regrets about my business, and without hesitation, I replied, "Only that I didn't start it *sooner!*"

While trucking was once considered a 'man's industry,' women are quickly becoming an integral part of this growing field in the US. Still though, we don't want to do our jobs well within our company 'for a woman;' but rather, we just want to 'do our jobs well – period.'

Hope and I work well together, each naturally picking up where the other leaves off. She prefers to drive during the day and then to go to sleep early, while I'm a 'night owl' and I enjoy driving through the night, under the stars, while it's peaceful, still and quiet.

One night, we'd driven straight through the night to our destination at a Dollar General. As always, Hope immediately began to unload our trailer onto the loading dock. She'd been sleeping all night while I drove, so she was feeling rested and ready to get to work.

"Wow! Hope's fast *for a woman!*" the receiving agent said as Hope hoisted merchandise and stacked pallets at the back of the trailer. "But, I'm not gonna kill myself for *nobody's* company!"

I just smiled and ignored his comment. It was clear that he'd never 'get it' and that he couldn't understand that Hope worked so hard because she wanted her *own company,* and so she felt responsible for every minute; every mile and every dollar. Even while we were still with Werner, we'd begun to think like business owners, and work like business owners. Business owners realize 'they ARE their business,' so their work and their reputation matter above all else.

It's a different type of responsibility to work for one's self, and there's a different sort of accountability too. There are no accolades; no favorable employee reviews and no pats on the back for a 'job well done.' Being an entrepreneur also means learning to be one's own biggest cheerleader.

But it's also a different sense of accomplishment and a different pay-off too. The satisfaction of entrepreneurship is different than one feels as an employee who does his singular job within an entire organization. It is visceral, intense and real – and no job, no title, no review, no kind words and no paycheck from another employer can *ever* top it.

After we'd set out on our own, Hope's previous employer, Werner, tried to get her to come back to the company. But after getting a taste of being her own boss, she wasn't interested in being an employee again. She'd learned a lot, and she's still thankful for her time there, but she's certain it was time to move on, expand her horizons and grow a bit as a person.

Like all things, truckers get out of their business what they put into it. Hope and I got used to running into other truckers and hearing them call us names like "The Money Makers." We've learned to make positives out of all situations though, and we even consider those comments to be compliments today, when we hear them. We like the fact that we're building a reputation for being dependable, hard workers.

As in all types of industries, and with all careers, it's important to stay knowledgeable about changes within the trucking industry. This pertains to everything, including changing regulations, laws, safety concerns, new equipment, technology, maintenance issues, billing methods and more.

I choose to keep myself motivated by reading books, attending seminars and staying on top of relevant trends and current developments. I vowed long ago, that I'd never be just another invisible African-American woman who didn't do anything with her life. My goal is to ensure that when I leave this Earth, that I've gotten out of my life every single ounce of success, enjoyment, satisfaction and happiness – and that I've done it *on my own terms.*

Chapter 5
Perspective & Positivity

Entrepreneurs have a different way of looking at the world and everything within it. While some people might look at an opportunity and think, "What will it *cost* me?" an entrepreneur looks at that same opportunity and thinks, "What will it *make* me?" To an entrepreneur, an opportunity is a vehicle to endless possibilities! *Their* job is to steer the vehicle along the way.

Successful entrepreneurs are generally positive people. They see 'the proverbial glass' as half-full and the world is bright with potential, in their eyes. Every new sunrise brings with it a new opportunity to do better, get ahead and move closer to success. And when they reach their goals and their successes, they create new ones and extend their reach a little more each time.

Entrepreneurs don't waste time with negativity. It is paralyzing and entirely useless. Their positive attitude is infectious, not only by nature, but also because people *want* to be around positive, productive people.

In my own quest to better myself, I choose to read and learn about self-improvement topics; financial opportunities; leadership strategies; motivational techniques; inspirational activities and entrepreneurial success stories, amongst other things. Everyone has something to share that can help another person and we can all learn through others – both through their successes and even their failures, which carry lessons too.

Entrepreneurs, like sharks, must keep moving forward in order to stay alive. Sharks must swim forward in the water because the motion forces water through their gills, which in turn, draws oxygen from the water and into their systems. If a shark *stops moving forward*, it will be unable to breathe and it will suffocate or drown and will likely be eaten by other sharks or predators. The same thing can be said of entrepreneurs. *They must keep moving or they'll drown.* So, even if he has a failure, a true entrepreneur doesn't just STOP; he keeps moving forward, armed with new lessons, as he follows his passion, one goal at a time.

The only real failures in life come when we don't try and when we fail to put forth the effort to better our selves and our lives. One thing holds people back from moving ahead and affecting change and it is the *fear of failure*. People fear the judgment of others if they should appear to fail. At the end of the day though, we only need the acceptance of one person – our selves. So, convince your *self* that it's okay to change your life, to reach and to extend your *self*; and then do it! Yours is the only opinion that matters! Yours is the only judgment that counts!

I've found that using a visualization technique makes it easier to 'put my self' *in* the life I desire. Take a moment to imagine, or *see*, yourself, just as you'd like to be in this life. Visualize the person you'd like to be if you could simply snap your fingers and change your circumstances, your life and your self. What does the 'new you' look like in your mind's eye?

Are you thinner and healthier?

Are you well dressed?

Do you dine at the best restaurants?

Are you free of stress and worry?

Do you live in your big, beautiful dream home?

Is your nice, new luxury car parked in the garage?

**Do you have plenty of time to spend with
your spouse or children?**

Is life fun?

Is your life organized & in order?

Do you have extra money saved?

Can you decide to go to the mall whenever you want?

Do you have plans & goals for the future?

Do you have extra money to donate to charity?

Are you able to attend your kids' games & recitals?

Have you built a solid and respected reputation for yourself?

Have you built a winning team?

Can you purchase a new car for you're your teenager?

Do you enjoy hobbies & recreation?

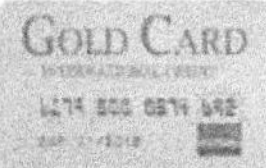

Are you free of credit card debt & obligations?

Do you take vacations?

Do you sleep well at night?

Are you excited every morning to wake-up and start the day to see what blessings, successes and accomplishments await you, like special gifts, just waiting to be unwrapped?

We're all different and so we all have different goals, aspirations and motivations for our selves and for our lives. Since we're all different, it's to be expected that we may not all want the same things out of life. But, whatever you may want, it IS within your reach and it's there for the taking! Decide to reach out, grab it and hold it in your grasp! Own it and make it yours!

In addition to visualization, successful people know the importance of putting themselves around others who are successful too. Positivity is infectious and it is easily multiplied. Immerse your self, heart, body and soul; and surround yourself with people who have similar interests, goals and motivations. Not only will this keep you motivated, but it will also help you to maintain your focus and to encourage you when times are tough. NO successful entrepreneur has had *only* successes in his life. The difference is that these people dare to try, to reach and to make their dreams a reality! They keep moving and growing; and they consistently reach a little higher and a little further than that which is within their comfort zone.

It's natural to place ourselves in the company of people whose ideals align with our own. This is exactly how it is with Hope and me; and it's the reason that our friendship and our business partnership work so well. We're both goal-oriented, success-drive, hardworking and forthright women who want the same things out of life. Ours is a comfortable partnership, built on faith and trust, and we each want the best for the other. It's a great gift to bask in the positivity and the potential of such a genuine friendship and it's one of the biggest reasons for our success. Simply put, we want the same things out of life and we're not afraid to work hard to get them.

Since we all have responsibilities and schedules to keep, it's not always possible to physically be surrounded by like-minded and motivated people. A secondary source of inspiration and motivation may easily and readily be found in magazines, books, podcasts and webinars. As humans, we're wired to digest positivity and automatically assimilate the motivating or inspirational information as it pertains to our *selves*.

Decide to be happy and to live in the light. Every day, wake-up with a light-hearted, happy attitude and watch how it affects every facet of your day, your business and your personal relationships. You'll observe a perpetual 'domino effect,' as one happy effect or experience naturally leads to the next and so on. You'll experience a better attitude, higher productivity and a lower stress level – all things that successful people enjoy in their daily lives.

A study at the University of Illinois at Urbana studied 'positivity and its effects as it correlates to success.' The study documented that there is definitely a 'happiness-success' link. The results of the study also revealed that happiness is associated with and precedes the vast majority of successful outcomes in life situations. With all the proof that happiness and a positive attitude fuel success, who *wouldn't* choose to ignite their own success by purposely living, day to day, with a happy attitude? Decide to be around inspirational, positive people; and when you can't be around them, at least read about them, their methods and their successes. And after you've reached the pinnacle of your own success, take the time to pass-on the positivity to someone else!

Chapter 6
What's the Secret?

As I began to do well in my business, I naturally was able to improve my lifestyle, one step at a time. Like many people, I'd aspired to have what some people might call 'the trappings of success.' I enjoyed the fact that I was able to afford the nice home, the new cars, the timeshare ownerships and vacations to places I'd once only read about. I'll admit that I enjoyed being able to afford to have and to do whatever I wanted. Instead of just reading travel magazines and imagining what it would be like to visit those places, I was there, enjoying them for my *self*.

"So, what's your *secret*, Lakeisha?" many friends and would ask.

I always laughed at this question, because the answer seemed so clear to me, that the question seemed unnecessary or even rhetorical. At times, I think people were actually disappointed that my answer was so simple –

and that it meant they'd have to actually DO something to achieve their own success.

"There's no *secret*," I'd explain again and again. "Hard work pays off. You'll get out of life what you're willing to put into it. No *secret* at all and it's available to everyone, just as it's available to *me*!"

While some people may have been inspired by my good work ethic and my success, I think others may have really wanted to believe there was some *secret* or some *magical potion* that would create a shortcut to success. It was as if it were easier for them to believe in these flimsy, fairytale possibilities, as opposed to acknowledging that 'hard work really does pay off.'

Even though Hope and I worked hard, day after day, especially in the earliest days of our business, I knew it was important to enjoy the fruits of our labor too. Having money and acquiring things is useless if we don't have time to enjoy them.

"Don't forget to LIVE!" I reminded my younger brothers one day when I talked to them about the importance of hard work. "We're not here, just to exist, until our time here is done. Take the time to enjoy all that you've worked for and to really LIVE!"

As their older sister, I feel it's my responsibility to expose my teenaged brothers to new experiences and new ideas, whenever possible. It's important to me that they know their possibilities in this life are infinite! I recently invited them to accompany me to Miami Beach where I attended Oprah's *The Life You Want Weekend*. While some people might not consider this to be a *vacation*, it was just *that* in my eyes. I basked in the positivity, good energies and inspiration for the entire weekend and I couldn't have been happier! And just like any other *vacation*, I was rejuvenated, recharged and revitalized after my time in Miami Beach! The spirit, the good vibes and the overall positivity were like a warm, welcome, cozy blanket – and I took it home with me, just like a treasured souvenir of my unique vacation!

Since I read for pleasure all the time, I often find interesting articles that pertain to business, success or just 'life in general.' It was not surprising to me to read about the importance of taking time 'off from work' from time to time. Studies show that our brains, as well as our bodies, need a vacation at times to rest, recharge, rejuvenate and re-power. Vacation time, of any kind, is a powerful and important tool that allows us to gain new insights, find refreshed perspectives and renew our spirits. By downshifting *(pun intended!)* and stepping outside of our professional roles, we gain a broader view of our roles within our company, within our families and within the world, as a whole.

Removing our selves from our familiar environments allows us a new, fresh perspective on our lives. Just like we consult with a close friend when we have a problem, stepping outside of our usual environment, allows us a bird's eye view of our own life and we see it more clearly. And by reaffirming the fact that we're a very small element of an infinite universe, we are reminded that there is indeed something much bigger than our selves. This affirmation keeps us grounded and gives us a healthy perspective of how we fit into our world.

But, just like a single raindrop in the gigantic ocean, we still have the power and the potential to affect others by our actions. This fact makes it critical that we decide to only affect others in a positive and productive way. After all, whatever we impose or project onto others is reflected back onto our selves. If we want to live in a positive light, we must first shine that light onto others for their benefit; and it then reflects back onto *us* again!

I try to keep this in mind when a friend or a family member comments on the fact that I seem to work all the time. "Don't you get tired of working all the time, Lakeisha?" they ask.

"No! Not at all!" I answer. "And I don't get tired of wanting things in life or wanting success either!"

I've finally realized that we all just don't want the same things out of life and we all don't require the same from our *selves*. We all set different standards for what we want and what we will allow; we all have our own aspirations; we set our own boundaries and have different comfort zones and we all have our own personal experiences that make-up whom we are today. Some people are willing to settle and to allow their circumstances and their previous experiences to define who they are and how far they will progress in life. But others don't choose to be held back by their pasts or burdened by previous experiences in their lives. For them, roadblocks and dead-ends do not exist as they make their way in the world and discover new things that make them stronger in the end. Their pasts do not define their present; nor do they impede their futures. As they move ahead, they are empowered when they turn around and realize how far they've come! And they are strengthened and propelled onward as they watch the gap widen, from where they began to where they are in life today. They view that 'gap' simply as a measure of their success and how far they've come!

All successful people have one thing in common: they look to themselves for change, advancement and signs they they're getting ahead. If things begin to seem stagnant, unproductive or too placid, don't look around at others for answers. Look into the mirror! The change begins with *you*!

Entrepreneurs know the importance of maintaining inspiration and this often comes from outside, external influences. Watch, listen and learn from others to gain inspiration and insight. And this doesn't mean to always replicate what you've observed. In fact, by watching and listening to others, you may find what 'not to do' based on what you learn from other people. Most people, especially those who have earned their success, are happy to share their own experiences, both good and bad; and there is tremendous value in learning from the mistakes of others. Why make the same mistakes, when we can avoid them, by learning what *not* to do? There is just as much value in learning from the mistakes and foibles of others, as there is in learning how to do things right!

Chapter 7
Invest in Your Self

Do you invest in stocks hoping to get a return on your initial investment? Do you invest time and money in making improvements to your home that increase it's value? Do you invest in your child's education to prepare them for their future and to give them a better life later? Well, it's exactly the same premise when we invest in our *selves* too.

Investing in yourself may mean exposing yourself to new business practices or new timesaving technology; this may save you time and make your business more efficient and more profitable. You may choose to invest in yourself by taking a few days off from your business to relax, recharge and refocus. This is a great investment in yourself because it will allow you to return to work with a refreshed outlook, a renewed spirit and clear head; all things that will benefit your production and let you work toward your goals. In the end, you've invested in yourself, since it is you who benefits.

Just like your employees, YOU are also your company's greatest asset. There is such a thing as 'human capital' and that is exactly what YOU are in the infrastructure of your business. YOU increase the value of your company's stock and YOU add value to how efficiently and profitably your company runs.

To increase the worth of your own 'human capital,' focus on building your competency, your knowledge and even your social and personality attributes. Simply be becoming more creative, more gregarious, more visible or more efficient, you will increase your 'human capital' and its economic value to your company.

Be sure to expand this to include your company's employees too, as they are also a huge asset; and if and when you sell your business, *they* will likely go with it, meaning *they* will be a part of the value that you can sell to a buyer. As a successful go-getter, *you* will be able to move on, take your 'human capital' with you and build another empire to sell!

So, 'how do you build your human capital?' you ask. It is a process and it requires dedication and focus. Basically, make the commitment to 'invest in your *self*.' Just as you invest money and time in other things, invest in your self through education, through experiences and by immersing yourself in situations in which you can learn and grow.

This may mean taking classes; obtaining certifications or new licenses; joining professional or trade organizations; becoming a Chamber of Commerce member; networking; learning about your competition; building a team; reading motivational books; attending seminars or conferences or visiting trade shows to learn about new products or technology that could benefit you and your company. As the owner of your business, you ARE your business. Any investment in YOU will therefore benefit your business.

Many people begin to find success and money and they choose to buy things that are 'wants' and not 'needs,' because they suddenly have disposable income. THIS is where some people begin to deviate on their path to financial freedom! When you come to this crossroad and have the ability to make impactful decisions, pause, breathe and make the most rational decision possible. Use that newfound money to 'invest in your self,' rather than purchasing a new car or a flashy Rolex watch. Buy new books, sign-up for an instructional course, attend a motivational seminar to better your self, give you new perspective and recharge your batteries!

I, personally, like to find an out of town seminar or conference, so I can parlay a few days of vacation time into my trip. This way, I can find motivation, reinvigorate myself and also relax a little too. By the time I return to work, I'm ready to take on the world and use what I've learned too. This way, I benefit, my business benefits and my customers also benefit!

Here's a helpful tip: After you've attended a seminar or educational workshop, set some goals for yourself that will allow you to use what you've learned. Actually write down your goals because this makes it more of a commitment and helps you to visualize your plan. Include a target date that will hold you accountable to your goals; and if they are long-term goals, also include short-term review points, so you'll be sure to keep yourself on track. Put the review dates and the target date in your planner or calendar. This will ensure that you see it, work toward it and make the goal a reality. Not only will you experience a sense of satisfaction as you see your progress, but your business will benefit and you'll increase the value of your 'human capital' in the process.

Chapter 8
With Purpose Comes Power

Have you ever known someone who just seems to glide through life on a wing and a prayer, with no real life goals or purpose? Have you observed him, as he simply exists in the world, day after day, with no real intentions, aspirations or purpose? His life is not full, if he simple exists; and he has no control and no power to direct his own life. He's simply 'along for the ride' and passively waiting to see what comes to him, day after day. Life and circumstances control *him* because he has no power over them or over himself.

If you sit back and think about *anyone* who has accomplished anything that's great or important, he has had an intensely focused drive, determination and **purpose.** His goal may have been to colonize a new land; develop a lifesaving vaccine; free an entire nation; create a new invention or heroically save a species, but his **purpose** was something far bigger than his intended goal. His purpose was likely to create opportunity for people; save lives; make life easier, more convenient or more efficient or even to save all of mankind, as we know it. It was because he *knew his intended purpose* that he accomplished his goal in the end. There is such value in identifying and unlocking our own purpose in life – as a professional, as a person and as a human being!

Goals are **not** *purpose*, not at all. Goals are things or end results that we wish to achieve and they are things or destinations that we work toward. *Purpose* is the 'why' and the 'reason' that we do what we do in this life. When we find, identify and unlock our unique purpose, we then know *why* we work, *why* we love and *why* we live. Knowing our purpose gives us incredible power in our lives!

In order to identify your own specific purpose, take time, all by your-self, to sit quietly and reflect. Purpose is a very personal, and even inti-mate, thing. Think about who you are; where you've been in your life; where you'd like to be in 10 years, 20 years and so on and WHY you'd like to be there. Chances are, you won't decide that you're here to 'make as much money as possible;' to 'have the biggest house in the neighborhood;' to 'drive the most expensive sports car' or to 'roll around in piles of cash' at your whim. Your *purpose* is more of the 'end result' of these things or goals. Your purpose is probably to live without stress, to create a comfort-able lifestyle for your family and to have the time to enjoy it. While your goals lead you to your purpose, they also support your purpose and pro-vide focus in everything you do.

Have you ever known a person who is always in a great mood, no mat-ter the situation or the circumstances? Does he seem to handle anything life throws at him, both good and bad, with authority and conviction? Is his reputation a positive one, both personally and professionally? Do his employees and co-workers seem to 'want to follow his lead,' work with him and support his goals and visions? This is because **he lives his passion** and it shows in everything he does in life!

Really think hard to identify your own purpose in this life and the ultimate reason for your very being and existence. To some, this may sound like an overwhelming endeavor; but if you'll ask yourself some simple questions, a picture will begin to form. You'll get a definitive lucid clarity about yourself and how you fit into this world.

There are no 'right or wrong' answers when you do this introspective exercise. It is only important that you be entirely honest – with yourself.

To identify your purpose, get out a sheet of paper, ask yourself the following questions and write down your answers, being as honest as possible:

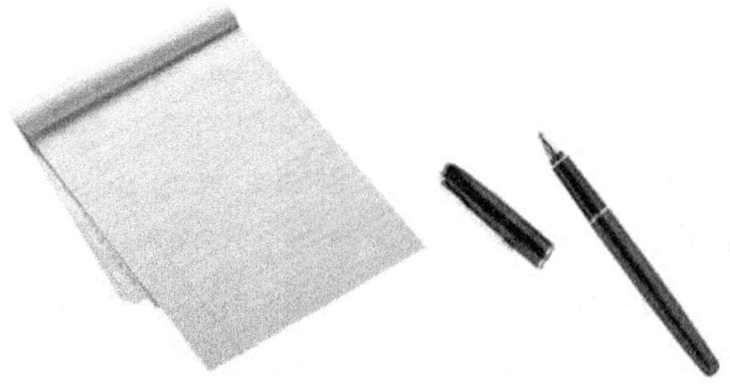

What excites you?

What specific gifts do you possess?

What sorts of things do people compliment you on or say you're 'good at?'

How do you spend your spare time?

Do people rely on you for certain things?

Is there a charity or a particular cause that is close to your heart?

What or whom inspires you most?

Do you have a certain expertise or specific skill?

Are you considered an expert in something?

Are you a take-charge overt person and a natural-born leader or more of a quiet, passive thinker?

The answers to these types of questions will reveal a lot about you and will begin to unlock your own *purpose* since they will show you the reason you do what you do in life. Your answers will reveal the reasons you set certain goals, the reasons for your aspirations and the overall motivation for your entire life.

Identifying your own unique purpose will give you a fierce and unstoppable power over your entire life!

This is because it brings with it a crystal clear, lucid focus that will keep you on your path to success. If you should ever stall or stumble, just realign with your purpose, and you'll instantly be back on track again.

Once you've finally identified your purpose in life, you will never again be the same! You will view life in two halves; as 'the time *before* I knew my purpose' and 'the time *after* I learned my purpose;' and this is because there will be a definitive difference in the 'new, enlightened you,' in the way you live, the way you view your life and the way others view you too. You'll embrace every facet of your life with a new perspective, a positive attitude and clear direction. You'll understand how to overcome obstacles, achieve goals, meet deadlines and create new, future goals and more. This is because you'll finally know your purpose, so you'll have a clear, defined destination in your mind of who you are and where you're going in life!

For most entrepreneurs, it is *not money* that they seek. Although their goal is to have wealth and to find success, their purpose is something altogether very different and it doesn't have dollar signs in it either. Many entrepreneurs will tell you that their *purpose* is to challenge themselves; to affect change; to have financial freedom; to create the best lifestyle possible for their families; to give back to the world or to prove to *themselves* that they 'can do it.' By reaching their goals, however, they in turn, *reinforce their purpose* and their reason for 'being.'

As soon as you start to live a life that's aligned with your overall *purpose*, many wonderful and positive things will immediately begin to happen. You'll have a clear focus and a concrete vision of the goals that support your purpose. You'll instantly be able to plan to achieve your goals, both short-term and long-term. Things will effortlessly and naturally begin to fall into place, both professionally and personally. You'll have a feeling of calm and a vivid clarity about life and your place within it. There will be a sense of peace like you've never before known. You will feel calm because you have focus and direction. All of these things will create an atmosphere that will allow you to move through your world with intention, confidence and peace. As a result, you'll be more productive, more efficient and more successful in all you do as you pursue your passion.

Finding and unlocking your own purpose not only benefits you, as a person, but it also benefits those around you. When others realize you know your purpose, they'll see you as a secure, focused leader. Your new found confidence will literally radiate from you and it will give others a sense that they should follow your lead an your example. They will naturally, sometimes even subconsciously, fall into step beside you to support your goals, which will in turn reinforce your overall purpose. The effect of knowing and unlocking your *purpose* is exponential and one of the most profound ways to better your whole life and to live your best life!

Chapter 9
Play, Live & Give

Although I'm older, I'm very close to my two teenaged brothers, ages 14 and 16; and I enjoy spending time with them, especially when I get to take them along with me on trips at times. Since I'm 12 and nine years old than my brothers, I sometimes naturally feel a sort of 'maternal responsibility' to them. My goal is to show them new things, expand their horizons and ignite a desire within them to want *even more* from their own lives. Nothing would make me happier or more proud than to see my brothers create amazing lives that are much more successful than my own!

It's important to me to show the boys that life is about responsibility and balance. They see me work a lot, so I make sure to let them see me enjoy some recreational times too. I want them to see firsthand the 'pay-off' of my hard work and all the hours I put in to my business.

Since I didn't have much training, as a teenager, about how to handle money or about finances in general. Money makes the world go round and it's a critical part of our lives. Teaching kids about it early will prepare them for their futures, once they step out into the world, on their own. I've always thought the high school curriculum should include mandatory classes on 'real world' things like how money works; our banking system; credit and its importance; budgeting and finance management. Kids would be much better prepared, as young adults, if they knew what to expect and how to handle things in the 'real world.'

"It's not just about making the money," I've explained to my brothers, "It's also about knowing how to handle it, once you get it."

Many people, even middle-aged adults, are inept at managing their own finances. While they may be dependable employees, who go to work day after day and bring home a paycheck, sometimes people are clueless about how to manage the money they've earned. This is the reason they never get very far in life – not because they don't earn enough, but because they don't realize that money is both a *tool* and a *vehicle* to their future. If they make it work for them, they can steer themselves right into a comfortable life! (If they don't know how to make money work though, they'll hit a dead-end or even sometimes totally derail from their course.)

I enjoy talking to my brother about money, what it means, what it can do and how to use it, once they have it. Elevating their knowledge prepares them and arms them for their futures, but I try not to make it overwhelming or boring, because I know I won't hold their attention. (And although the Bible has 2,350 verses relating to finances, I never *preach* to them! It wasn't so long ago, that I was a teenager myself and I know they'll tune me out if I begin to preach!)

Sometimes we play games with money, we read and we talk the subject. My 16-year old brother plays basketball, and loves school. I'm always amazed by our conversations! My 14-year old brother loves soccer, and wants to be on a SWAT team one day. He, too, amazes me when we all sit and talk! While only a few guys turn out to be world-class athletes, ALL of them must deal with money in their everyday lives. No matter what they do in life though, 'money' and 'finances' will play an important role in how they live.

To teach kids about money, they first must understand that money is a commodity that is earned and not just given freely. This places a value on it and creates certain expectations and a sense of responsibility and ownership. Allowing kids to have some freedom with their own money will also teach them how to handle it.

Assign age-appropriate chores to children and then pay them when they successfully do those chores. If, however, they fail to properly do them, or if they don't do them in the required timeframe, you must *not* pay them. It'll be a lesson that's much easier learned under the tutelage of family, than out in the cold, harsh real world. Kids need to understand that when they do a poor job or if they fail to 'show up for work on time,' that they won't be paid. And as difficult as it may be, stand firm on this. If your son had been saving to buy a new $50 video game, but he failed to wash the family car, don't give in and hand over the final $10 he needs! Love him enough to guide and teach him responsibility and cause and effect!

Because money is a tool, teach kids how to use it and what it can do. Show them how money is used to live, to play and to help others. Once kids begin to understand the various uses for money, they'll also start to realize they must learn to budget their money and stretch it to meet certain goals. Kids that are only taught to 'save every penny,' really don't have a clear understanding of money or finances. When they become adults, all they'll know is 'how to save' the money they've earned. But those who learn that money is used to **live, play and give**, have a better 'whole, well-rounded understanding' of money and what it does in the world. When teaching kids to budget their money, always allow them a little 'play' money to spend at their discretion. They need to reap the reward for earning their money; they'll learn reasoning and decision-making skills and they'll feel a sense of accomplishment. It's all part of the broad teaching plan of how to handle money.

When kids get old enough, decrease their allowance and encourage them to find a part-time job to earn money. This creates an autonomy and forges a personal relationship for them with 'their own money.' Having a 'real employer' will give kids a sense of freedom and it will foster their independence, as they prepare to live in the 'real world.'

Kids of all ages take their cues from the adults around them. For this reason, it's critical to remember that kids are always watching us. They see what we do, how we behave and how we react to situations. There's nothing wrong with allowing kids to see you pay your monthly bills or with telling them they'll 'have to wait till next week for that new pair of $80 shoes' they just *have* to own. It's a good thing for kids to know you save all year for your family's summer vacations. And it's a positive lesson when kids know you have to tap your 'savings reserve' when faced with an unexpected car repair. ***IT'S LIFE***. And kids need to be exposed to LIFE, before they're responsible for their *own life* and their parents are no longer around.

No matter where your family falls on the socio-economic scale, there is always someone who has needs beyond your own. Kids need a sense of where they fall in society, so they'll also learn to help those less fortunate than themselves. Make it a practice to help others, no matter how little money or time you can give. Kids will learn compassion, empathy and responsibility when they see their parents helping others, donating money or physically helping those in need. People are always judged by *how they treat those that are weakest in society*. Prepare your kids to treat others, as they'd also like to be treated.

Show kids how money works by letting them know what you do for a job and how you earn a living. When you get paid, show them how you budget your earnings and how you pay your bills. They need to see and understand the relationship you have with your money, how you use it, the power and potential it has and how it affects your life and theirs.

Chapter 10
See It, Say It, Be It, Make It

If you want others to see you as a successful and valuable person, then you must first see *yourself* in this same way. Many things may be out of your control, but there are a few things that can be steered, directed and created. Your own image and how 'the world sees you' is one of those things.

Studies have shown that people make-up their minds about others and form an opinion of them in from 1.5 to 7 seconds! It's much more difficult to reverse someone's opinions of us than it is to give them a good first impression, right from the start. And this benefits YOU on every level.

After you've identified your purpose, set some goals and dedicated yourself to working harder than ever before, you must begin to put yourself in the position where you aspire to be. Imagine for a moment what a 'successful YOU' looks like.

Are you professionally dressed, organized and neat? Do you have a dependable reputation as someone who can be relied upon and counted upon, day and night? Whatever the image of a 'successful YOU' may be, is exactly how you want to see yourself and exactly how you should portray yourself to the world. Even IF you haven't reached the pinnacle of your success yet, you can still 'look the part.' It's the first step to creating your new reality! **SEE** your self as the success you'd like to be!

Don't listen to negativity from anyone – ever. The thoughts and opinions of others, if they're not supportive of you and your purpose, are a waste of time and energy. Ignore them and focus only on fulfilling your purpose. There will be some days when it's more difficult than others to hold onto your vision of the 'successful YOU.' Circumstances may get in the way, problems might arise and daily stressors can creep into your world. It's on these days, that you'll have to hold on even tighter to your initial vision of the 'successful YOU." When the going gets tough, step away, stand in front of a mirror and remind yourself that you'll get through the day and that you'll make it. Literally **SAY** IT in order to reinforce it in your mind!

After you've 'walked the walk' and 'talked the talk' long enough, you'll begin to notice a change in yourself. You'll walk taller; you'll speak with confidence; you'll hear conviction in your own voice and you'll notice other people watching you, listening to you and relying on you for your input, your opinions or your direction. This is because others have recognized and 'bought into' the image of the new 'successful YOU.'

We actually *teach others how to treat us*, based upon how we regard ourselves. If we were to arrive at work in a disheveled state, with wrinkled clothes, 'bed head' hair and scuffed shoes, our appearance sends a clear message to all who see us. That message loudly says: *'I'm not worth it. I don't care about myself. I have no self-respect; so there's no reason you should care about me or respect me either!'*

On the other hand, if we arrive at work or for an appointment 'on time;' neatly and professionally dressed; fresh-faced and impeccably groomed and with an attitude of 'I've got it all together,' people immediately have a favorable opinion of us. Our image sends the message that we are dependable, organized and orderly; and that 'we care about our selves,' so others should too. This favorable image makes it much easier to convince customers to take a chance on you; employees to follow your lead and people, in general, to treat you with respect.

If we have self-respect and if we maintain our dignity, others will pick-up on these things and they will also treat us with dignity and respect. If we groom ourselves and dress ourselves with care, it shows the world that 'we count' and 'we're worth the time it takes' to put ourselves together. Since others will perceive that we value our personal appearance and the outward persona we show to the world, they will also value us. If we speak intelligently and articulately, it not only speaks volumes for our intelligence; it also says we care about how we communicate and the messages we deliver. If our office, our car and our home are tidy, organized and clean, it silently and subconsciously sets an expectation in others about what they can expect from us.

An orderly image portrays a picture of someone who is responsible, disciplined and efficient. This image is great for customers to see, since it gives them a glimpse of what to expect from you and your company. It's equally positive for employees to view too, because it shows them what you deem to be acceptable and it subliminally sets expectations for them of your tolerances. Make the decision to show the world how to treat you by allow them to make certain inferences about you. In other words, **BE** the 'successful you' that you want to be!

The process of creating one's own success is done in steps. After you've envisioned yourself as a success; reminded yourself that you are indeed a success and lived your life as a success, it will become second nature to you and you'll no longer think about it. It's at this point, that you'll recognize a major shift in the person who looks back at you from the mirror. And it's also at this point that you'll realize people treat you differently and regard you differently. You'll notice they seem to have an elevated perspective of the new 'successful you.' This is not because you've perpetrated the perfect genius hoax. And it's not because you're pretending to be someone or something that you are not. It's simply because you have become the 'successful you' that you first envisioned! You've **MADE** it!

It's a simple process to create the new, successful you! Just **SEE** it; **SAY** it; **BE** it and then **MAKE** it!

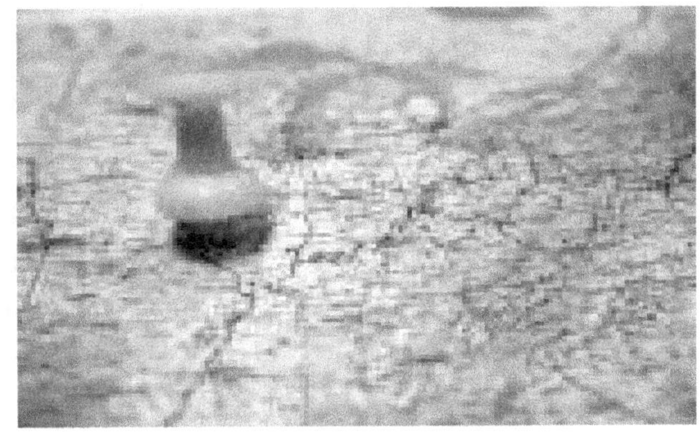

Chapter 11
Maps & Mentors

Just as we use maps and GPS to get to our destinations in our work, I also like to have a plan and to know where I'm going in life. Without a plan, I'd simply languish, marking time, with no specific purpose – and that's pointless, in my view.

We are the writers of our own lives and if we want to have a great story, then we need to take some responsibility for it and make it a good one. What goes around in life always comes back around again. This is why it's so important to treat people with respect in all things. Every person in our life has something of value to offer and share, even if we don't immediately recognize it. Look at Lillie Drennan, for instance, all the way back in 1929. I've never even met her, and yet she's positively impacted my life and my future by paving the way for females in the trucking industry. We never know how our action will affect others, now or in the future. Personally, I hope to have only a positive impact on the world, so I live my life treating others as I want to be treated and respecting everyone in my world.

So many people know what they want out of life, but they have no idea of how to attain it. No one gets anywhere though, without taking the first step. With all the inspiring success stories out there, there's a role model for each of us. But, even more than a role model, it is recommended that people find a mentor to help them to their goals.

All mentors have different relationships with their mentees or protégés. It's dependent upon their objectives, their career paths and their specific needs. The role of a mentor is not necessarily one of friendship, but since a good mentor wants the best for his mentee, a friendship often is formed. Through a mutual trust and respect, a mentor helps to propel his mentee forward; he shares his own knowledge and skillset; offers advice; helps with goal-setting; suggests resources; gives career advice; makes introductions; assists with networking and helps his mentee to maintain his focus. The best mentors are genuine cheerleaders who want only the best for their protégés.

Finding a mentor is a very personal exercise. This is because the mentor-mentee relationship is like none other. A mentor is not a best friend, not a parent and not a spouse. He is sometimes a placid observer and sometimes an integral participant with his mentee. But he always keeps the best interests of his mentee at the forefront of their relationship.

Depending upon one's objectives or goals, their desired career path, their industry and their personal needs, the process of finding a mentor can be simple or difficult. For instance, a student may ask his professor to mentor him; an employee may ask his boss to mentor him; an alcoholic may ask his AA sponsor to mentor him or a runner may ask a marathon winner to mentor him. It all depends on the circumstances and the personal needs of both mentor and mentee.

Never be afraid to ask a person to mentor you. Chances are, he has had a mentor too, at one time or another in his life or his career. And most people are flattered to be asked to have such a defining and important position in the life of another.

Statistics show that having a mentor boosts the careers of successful mentees. Unlike a typical network contact, in which you might shake hands, exchange business cards and maybe a phone call, the mentor-mentee relationship extends far beyond that scene. A good mentor will be 'in your corner' and 'on your side' in all things, but he will also provide an objective opinion and guidance when necessary.

It's not as difficult as it may seem to find a mentor today. Thanks to social networking, you can actually find many mentors right at your fingertips. And again, thanks to today's advanced technology, you can even meet with your mentor from the comfort of your own home and in front of your computer screen at a mutually convenient time.

A mentor is usually in a position that you'd like to one day be in too. Since he's accomplished the goal of rising to your desired position, he is certainly qualified to help you to get there too. Select someone you admire and respect, both personally and professionally – after all, we are *the sum of all our parts* – and for entrepreneurs, especially, our personal and professional lives often merge. You may already know your potential mentor or you may have never been introduced. Either way, the arrangement can work. But, do your homework first, before approaching your potential mentor. You should know all about him, his platforms, his beliefs, his ambitions, his preferred charities, his career history and the organizations with which he's affiliated, etc. before you ever contact him! This information will be invaluable to you as you approach your potential mentor; and he will appreciate that you've done your homework and have put some effort into your plight because it's important to you. Your efforts will garner respect and will start-off your mentor-mentee relationship on the right track.

Some people find it difficult to ask their direct supervisors to be their mentors. This is because it's best to be able to speak freely and to easily share your opinions with your mentor. This is sometimes difficult to do when speaking to one's own supervisor.

While most people choose a mentor who has 'in their eyes' already reached the pinnacle of his success, others sometimes find great value in being mentored by someone 'at their own level.' This is, once again, because we all have something to teach, based on our own experiences and perspectives! A 'lateral-level mentor' can also relate better to a mentee's current problems, obstacles, frustrations and desires.

People sometimes choose to use a life coach as their mentor too. A life coach is a professional that is hired to help clients to identify their passions, set goals, and achieve personal and professional successes. The role of a life coach is to provide guidance, motivation and encouragement as aligned with each client's needs and goals. Finding the right life coach can completely change and enhance your life!

Some people choose to have multiple mentors throughout their lives and their careers. This is because they're constantly moving up, getting ahead and setting new goals as they pursue their own passions. As needs change, so can your mentor or your life coach!

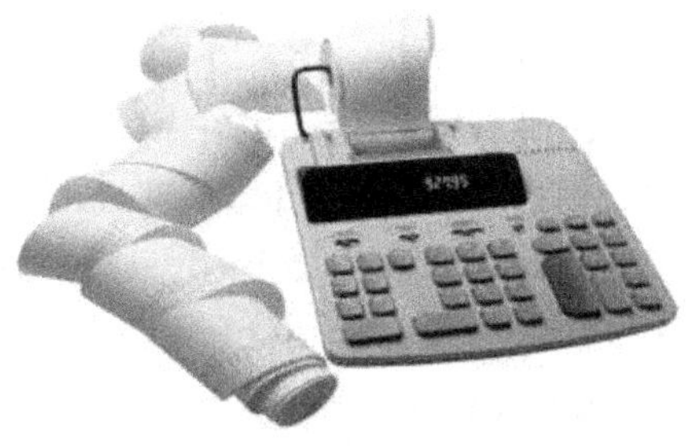

Chapter 12
Budgets & Blinders

Have you ever noticed a sign on the back of a long trailer that read: *'If you can read this, then you're too close; driver can not see you in his blind spot'*? Truck drivers contend with numerous blind spots while driving their rigs, simply by design. But, because they're aware the blind spots exist, they take extra precautions to protect the safety of other drivers as well as them selves. Lives would be lost if truck drivers simply drove along blindly and ignored the fact that blind spots exist all around their loaded 80,000-pound rigs. Truck driver training teaches new drivers how to identify their blind spots, constantly check them and make evasive safety maneuvers when required.

The same can be said of taking care of our own finances, both personally and within our businesses too. If we went through life, *blindly* living in it, and with no regard for what happens around us, accidents will surely occur and lives may even be devastated because of our oversight and poor choices.

Just as truck drivers carefully check and maintain their rigs, we also must apply this same precautionary and preemptive thinking to the management of our money. We have a safety checklist for our rigs and so we should have a list, or a budget, with which to manage our finances too.

Just the *word* 'budget' sometimes throws people into a tailspin. But, when they do this, they abruptly apply their brakes and jack-knife their plans, which only delays their progress. Some people don't want to take the time to create a budget, while others simply don't know HOW to do it. Either way, budgets are a great tool that shows us how we use our money and how we can adjust or plan to use it best.

Budgets give us a practical and tangible look at our finances and they help us to get a grip on what's coming in and what's going out each week; each month and each year. A budget can be very simple or it can be very elaborate, depending on your needs, your objectives and your resources.

First, identify how and where you spend your money. Make a list of all the things you spend money on each month, from your mortgage; to you car payment; to credit card payments, groceries and dry-cleaning -- and even those tasty Starbucks coffees that we all love. Review your list and note how you spend your hard-earned money. Sometimes, this exercise, *in itself*, is very illuminating and eye opening! You'll definitely identify some expenditures that are really luxuries and not necessities in your life. You will also visibly identify places from which you are 'leaking cash.' In this case, if your goal is to *save* more money, you'll see that you can cutout these unnecessary expenses and 'stop the leaking!'

Spending above our limits is very dangerous and it's also a prime cause for many couples' lives being ruined. If the financial burden doesn't destroy them, then the stress certainly will! Review your expenses as the first step to creating your budget.

Next, look at your overall monthly *net* income. Include every source of money that provides *dependable* liquid cash to you. This includes all wages; tips; dividends; alimony; child support payments, etc.

Step Three to creating your budget is to add together your monthly expenditures; then add together your monthly income and then subtract your expenditures from your income. Hopefully, you still have a positive figure left over, as this is the amount you have left after you've paid all your bills each month. This figure is the money you should save or invest each month.

It is also advisable to put away extra cash as a 'cushion' in the event you have unexpected expenses like vehicle repairs, illness, emergencies and unforeseen situations. This 'cushion' will also act as a safety net, in the event you suddenly lose your job or have your hours cut at work, which adversely affects your income. A reserve 'cushion' may provide the only lifeline you'll have when dealing with life's unexpected surprises!

TIP: Each month, when paying your bills, 'pay yourself' first, and put away money in a savings or reserve account. If this is done regularly, it will become a positive habit, and the day will come when you'll be thankful for this extra money.

While it's not always easy to adjust and increase one's income, we *can* adjust our spending habits and control some of our expenditures. A budget will visually highlight the individual areas in which you can curtail your spending. Little things add up quickly! For instance, if you 'brown bag' your lunch, even *once a week*, instead of eating out, you can save $40 - $50 at the end of the month or $480 - $600 in a year. If you decide to take your morning coffee with you, instead of buying it on the way to work each day, you can save $15 a week, $60 a month and $720 a year. If you do both of these suggestions, you'll have an extra $1,200 to $1,300 at the end of the year to spend on Christmas gifts or to put into your vacation account. It's the little changes, the tiniest drops of water in the vast 'ocean of finances' that ultimately have a huge effect on our lives and our overall lifestyles. Even the smallest changes have a noticeable ripple effect!

It takes some skill and good judgment to shift a 10-speed semi truck, and most people don't know how to simply jump up into the cab and drive such a complicated, monstrous machine. Therefore, it stands to reason that learning to budget, and to handle something as all-important as money, also takes practice and proper training. Budgets are not set in stone either, and may be changed or adjusted, as circumstances and goals change. A budget is meant to be a visible guide and a checks-and-balance system for managing finances, both for individuals and for corporations.

Also known as a transport truck, a semi-trailer truck is a gigantic vehicle that consists of a towing engine commonly called a *tractor*. The tractor is a very necessary component in the trucking industry and without it, many people would be dead in the water, commerce would cease, the economy would implode and freight would not move. It's THAT important! Consider your *budget* as your own tractor. You will be attached to it, just as a trailer is attached to the tractor, and you must learn to check it regularly, maintenance it, make adjustments as needed and realize that you 'each needs the other to properly do the job!' And while you may sleep in your tractor, tucked away comfortably in a sleeper cabin, you will only rest well if you're sure your tractor and your trailer is properly and safely maintenance, just like you'll sleep better if your budget is in good shape and your finances properly maintenance too.

Chapter 13
Living With Intent & Finding Wealth

I've chosen to live my life with intent. Everything I do in life, I do with the intent that I will prosper from it in some way. This may not always mean digits in my bank balance either! Sometimes, I prosper as a person and as an individual, when I grow as a person from an experience. I've learned that there is great value in that too!

The past is behind me, so I choose to move ahead and to 'be the generation of change.' This doesn't mean that everything comes easy. In fact, some things can be very difficult at times.

My goals, my success, and even my early failures, have taught me to prioritize my life and to create my plan for what I want out of this life. Like so many young people, I once thought that if I 'just had plenty of money,' that I'd have it all! I worked had, banked plenty of money – and then blew it all. *Yes, I foolishly blew it all!*

Nothing will take the wind out of your sails like working like crazy and then realizing 'it's all gone.' It was 2008 and I'd gotten my first apartment with my best friend, Hope, in Tampa. At the time, I was in school and working toward my certification as a pharmacy tech and also working part-time at Sally's Beauty Supply as an assistant manager and key holder.

Hope and I worked every week, but then we blew our whole paychecks on the weekends. Sometimes, we even gave money to friends or family who needed help, but our paychecks only went so far. This created some major problems, of course, as we tried to figure out our newfound 'adult world.'

We learned very quickly that it's very difficult to navigate through life without money! In fact, it's almost paralyzing and the constant sense of panic makes for many sleepless nights and a sickening sense of nausea that doesn't go away. It's almost as if 'money' were a drug and once we'd gotten it, we temporarily felt better – until it was all gone again, much too soon, and then the sickening process started all over again. It was a cycle that I hated.

I also hated the feeling of being broke. One Saturday, we were so broke that we had only a few hotdogs in our refrigerator. Since we had no ketchup, Hope and I had to scrape together enough coins to go and buy a small bottle of ketchup. We looked for loose coins in purses; in kitchen drawers; in our cars and in any other nook and cranny we could find. When we'd found enough coins, we went to Wal-Mart and purchased a bottle of ketchup. It was a humiliating feeling as I counted out my coins and then handed them over to the cashier; and watched her count them again as other customers impatiently watched and waited behind me. When Hope and I got back to our apartment, that hotdog had never tasted so awful to me after the humiliation I'd just experienced! In fact, *life* didn't taste too good at all either on that fateful day!

I vowed that I had to do something to change my circumstances if I was to ever improve my own life. It was up to me. There was really no one whom I could even call for advice or solace at that time. I felt like a woman, alone on an island, as the tide came in, threatening to swallow me up and drown me. I knew it would be up to me to change things if I wanted my life to amount to something more.

It wasn't long after 'the ketchup episode' that I learned I didn't pass the pharmacy tech exam; and I found that I'd have to wait a whole year to take it again. But now, as I look back, that was all really a blessing in disguise, because it's at that time that I began to consider a career in trucking that would lead to entrepreneurial success; and with Hope's urging I decided to go for it.

It was also the time that I decided to live my life with intent and to follow my passion. This meant that I'd also have to learn to 'say no' to people and to make some sacrifices as I stuck to my plan to get ahead and build a life for myself. I make sure I have options in my life today, because with options, I also have opportunity and choices.

Some people fear change, but change is actually a good thing. It means you're *moving*. If water were still and not moving, we couldn't drink it because it wouldn't be clean. The same is true of life; it must keep moving so we can use it and enjoy it. But if we ever don't like our circumstances, we can simply change them. Sometimes changing our life is harder than others, but with hard work and determination, it's always possible. And all we really need is 'the possibility.'

Getting too comfortable means you're not moving and therefore not growing in life or as a person. *Comfort kills dreams* because it can be paralyzing! I've learned to embrace and even *welcome* change now, because with change, I am moving and so there is progress. And isn't that what life is all about – about progressing, changing and growing?

I am convinced that just because others may not share my same specific ambitions, that it's still okay for me to have them. They're MINE and this life is MINE. And I intend to get out of it all I can while I'm here!

Today, I live my life with intention as I follow my passion and take my place among about 200,000 other female semi drivers on the highways, riding high above the cars and eyeing my future on the horizon. My passion, however, is not just to *drive a big rig*. My *passion* is to work for my self; to control my own destiny; to create my own opportunities and build my future; to have financial freedom; to see the country on my own terms and to *enjoy my life*, both one day and one mile at a time. I now know that 'the money' that I thought I *had to have* is not 'the end goal,' not at all. The money is only *the vehicle* that allows me to work my plan, follow my passions and to achieve my dreams in this life.

It's been said that '**some people are so poor that all they have is money.**' I know exactly what that means. Today I have a newfound clarity and I know exactly how and where I fit into this life. I've had the nice cars, the impressive homes and the expensive vacations. But *nothing* is as gratifying as owning my own business, controlling my life, enjoying my freedom and *giving back and sharing it* with others so they, too, can have it and enjoy their own lives!

THAT is the **wealth** that I love being able to share!

Chapter 14
LINE HAUL LIFE LESSONS

A 'line haul driver' is a professional who drives an 18-wheeler from one point to another, or from Point A to Point B, with no stops in between and with only one goal and one focus: *to deliver the goods*. All people, no matter their passion, the industry they serve or their current station in life, can develop the same focus too, as they steer their own lives along their roads to success.

Determine your destination point, or your final goal, map out the best route to follow and navigate to your own Point B in life, one mile at a time. Before you embark on your journey, ensure that your vehicle (aka your *self*) is in optimum shape and properly maintained so there will be no breakdowns along the way. Make sure you have enough cash to hold you over until you reach Point B and reap the rewards of your successful journey. Observe the 'rules of the road' and the laws, so you'll build a solid reputation and good character along the way. Don't take detours or shortcuts, in hopes of getting there sooner; you may only get lost! If you come upon some speed bumps along the way, just slow down and then proceed with caution as you go right over them. Check your mirrors and be aware of what's around you, but focus on what's in front of you and where you're headed. Don't pick-up extra riders who may distract you along the way. Don't pick-up additional cargo or baggage that will only weigh you down and delay your arrival time. When you come upon other slower vehicles (aka people) along your road to success, don't just slow down and stay behind them; pass them and continue on your journey, because YOU are the leader who sets the pace and the one others should follow! And when you finally pull into your Point B 'destination of success,' don't slide in sideways with tires burning and horns blaring to call attention to the fact that 'you've MADE IT.' Cruise in, with dignity and decorum, on time and on-schedule, with your stellar reputation preceding you and announcing your arrival. Trust me, people will quietly notice that you've MADE IT! And don't be surprised if some of them ask, *"What's your secret? What route did you take? Can you teach* me *how to navigate like you do? How did you avoid delays and obstacles; and will you show* me *how to do it too?"*

Because education is a fluid and ever-changing concept, I'm still learning as I go through this thing called *life* – and I think it's a good thing, since I plan to continue to evolve as I set new goals that allow me to pursue my passions. Thanks to some things I've learned along my own road to success, and even some mistakes I've made too, I've collected some valuable tidbits, lessons and words of wisdom that might be helpful to others as they drive toward their own successes.

Following is a list lessons and inspirations that I've found helpful over the years and that I hope will benefit others too, as they maintain their focus and follow their passions, just like the best line haul drivers on their road to success:

TRUST YOUR INSTINCTS IN ALL CIRCUMSTANCES.

DON'T ASSUME EVERYONE IS YOUR FRIEND.

ALWAYS STAY GROUNDED.

STAY FOCUSED & YOU'LL FIND HAPPINESS & SUCCESS.

DON'T GET TOO COMFORTABLE – COMFORT KILLS DREAMS.

IF YOU DON'T LIKE YOUR LIFE – CHANGE IT.

EMBRACE CHANGE – IT BRINGS OPPORTUNITY.

WORK HARDER THAN EVERYONE ELSE.

ENTREPRENEURSHIP GIVES YOU ENDLESS OPTIONS.

DO SOMETHING DAILY THAT SUPPORTS YOUR DREAMS.

IF THE BIG PICTURE SEEMS SCARY, THEN JUST LOOK AT SMALL PIECES AT A TIME OF THE BIG PICTURE.

FIND A MENTOR OR A LIFE COACH.

LEARN SOMETHING NEW EACH DAY.

MAKE INFORMED DECISIONS.

'NO' IS AN ANSWER THAT NEEDS NO EXPLANATION.

DIFFICULT DAYS ARE ONLY SPEED BUMPS IN THE ROAD OF LIFE; SLOW DOWN, BUT KEEP GOING.

DON'T FEAR SUCCESS.

ANYTHING IS POSSIBLE IF THERE IS DESIRE.

HAVE THE COURAGE TO BUILD THE BEST LIFE.

DREAM BIG & WORK HARD.

DON'T WORRY ABOUT THE OPINIONS OF OTHERS.

PERSEVERANCE + PATIENCE = A PAYDAY

IF OTHERS DID IT, THEN SO CAN YOU.

A PROBLEM IS JUST ANOTHER CHANCE TO LEARN.

EXCUSES ARE UNPRODUCTIVE.

SAY WHAT YOU THINK; BUT THINK WHAT YOU'LL SAY.

NEVER FLY SO HIGH YOU CAN'T SEE FROM WHERE YOU CAME.

YOU CAN'T LOSE IF YOU'RE STILL IN THE GAME.

WORK HARD, PLAY HARDER & ALWAYS GIVE BACK.

WORRYING IS ONLY A USELESS WASTE OF ENERGY.

IF YOU GET SCARED, TAP THE BRAKES, BUT DON'T STOP.

PROGRESS BEGINS WITH THE FIRST STEP.

THE ONLY FAILURE IS IN NOT TRYING.

KEEP MOVING OR YOU'LL PERISH.

WE ALL HAVE SOMETHING OF VALUE TO SHARE.

PEOPLE FORGET THE PAIN, BUT THEY REMEMBER THE PRIDE.

IF YOU DON'T LIKE YOUR DREAM, CREATE A NEW ONE.

PERFECTION IS A MYTH.

POSITIVE PEOPLE PROGRESS PRIDEFULLY.

ATTITUDE IS INFECTIOUS.

BE MINDFUL OF HOW YOU TREAT EVERYONE.

LIVE YOUR LIFE FOR YOURSELF.

DECIDE TO THRIVE.

SHOW OTHERS THE WAY IF THEY STUMBLE.

SUPPORT YOUR PASSION WITH EVERY ACTION.

SURROUND YOURSELF WITH LIKE-MINDED PEOPLE.

CLASS & INTEGRITY CAN'T BE BOUGHT.

LEARN FROM THOSE WHO ARE DIFFERENT.

SUCCESS IS A TEAM SPORT – NO ONE FINDS IT ALONE.

LAUGH – EVEN AT YOURSELF.

THE ONLY WRONG DECISION IS NO DECISION AT ALL.

PASSION FUELS SUCCESS, BUT GOALS ARE THE MILE MARKERS.

SHINE YOUR LIGHT & SHARE YOUR SPIRIT.

EVERYONE HAS THE POWER BUT ONLY SOME HAVE THE WILL.

DON'T TALK ABOUT IT – GO AND DO IT.

PACE YOURSELF IN THE RACE & TAKE TIME TO BREATHE.

ANGER CHANGES NOTHING.

ON YOUR WORST DAY, SOMEONE ELSE IS DYING.

DREAMS CAN CHANGE AS WE CHANGE TOO.

GRAB LIFE LIKE IT'S THE LAST CHOCOLATE CHIP COOKIE!

CHOOSE TO LET GO OF THE PAST.

ASPIRE – INQUIRE – ACQUIRE – REQUIRE - and then repeat.

WE'RE JUDGED BY HOW WE TREAT THE WEAKEST.

BE YOURSELF IN ALL THINGS.

HONEST PEOPLE SLEEP WELL.

RESPECT CAN'T BE BOUGHT & IS WORTH EVERYTHING.

OBSTACLES ONLY MEAN WE'LL PUSH HARDER & REACH HIGHER.

DON'T WAIT TO CHANGE YOUR LIFE.

TEACH OTHERS HOW THEY SHOULD TREAT YOU.

TO GAIN RESPECT, WE MUST FIRST RESPECT OURSELVES.

EVERYONE IS NOT MOTIVATED BY THE SAME THINGS IN LIFE.

DREAMS ARE AS DIFFERENT AS THE DREAMERS.

DO EVERYTHING 100% AND WITH ALL YOUR HEART.

MISTAKES LEAVE LESSONS IN THEIR WAKE.

NEVER COMPROMISE.

WE EARN OUR LIVING; WE'RE BLESSED WITH OUR LIFE.

LEARN TO LIKE YOURSELF.

IF YOU NEED TO DIET, JUST FORGIVE SOMEONE; YOU'LL IMMEDIATELY FEEL LIGHTER.

CREATE POSITIVE HABITS.

WINNERS ARE MADE – SELF-MADE, THAT IS.

VISUALIZE THE 'SUCCESSFUL YOU' AND SHARE THAT VISION.

SUCCESS CAN SEEM LONELY – UNTIL EVERYONE HEARS YOU'VE MADE IT.

PROBLEMS ARE POTHOLES THAT CAN BE PATCHED.

PROCEED WITH CAUTION; JUST KEEP MOVING FORWARD.

CHARACTER IS INVISIBLE AND YET IT LEAVES THE BIGGEST IMPRESSION OF WHO WE ARE.

ALWAYS HAVE A PLAN FOR TOMORROW.

THIS LIFE IS YOUR SHIP AND YOU ARE THE CAPTAIN.

EVEN ONE DROP OF WATER FOREVER CHANGES AN OCEAN.

WHEN SUCCESS IS THE DESTINATION, THERE IS NO SHORTCUT.

FIND YOUR PASSION AND IGNITE YOUR LIFE.

IF YOU'RE ONLY WORKING FOR THE MONEY, YOU'LL NEVER FEEL FULFILLED -- NO MATTER *HOW* MUCH MONEY YOU HAVE.

COMMIT TO MEMORY THAT FIRST FEELING OF PRIDE AND REMEMBER IT ON THE TOUGHEST DAYS.

WORK IS A VERB.

DISCOVER SOMETHING NEW EVERY DAY.

INSPIRATIONS + MOTIVATIONS = GREAT VACATIONS

IT TAKES COURAGE TO BE DIFFERENT.

SOME PEOPLE WATCH FOR CHANGE, WHILE OTHER PEOPLE MAKE THE CHANGES.

LIVE WITH INTENTION; PLAN WITH INSIGHT.

GUILT & SHAME ARE HEAVY, WHILE PURITY & FORGIVENESS ARE LIGHT. RELEASE YOUR BURDENS.

INCREASE THE VALUE OF YOUR 'HUMAN CAPITAL.'

WORK ON YOUR BUSINESS AND NOT JUST 'IN' IT.

OWN YOUR BUSINESS; DON'T LET IT OWN YOU.

SUCCESS LEAVES THE BEST LASTING LEGACY.

I'll see you along the Road to Success!

Please be sure to honk & wave!

Your Friend in Success,

Lakeisha